PROSPERO'S LIBRARY

The Book of Symbols

Magic

CHRONICLE BOOKS

SAN FRANCISCO

First published in the United States in 1995 by Chronicle Books.

Copyright © 1994 Duncan Baird Publishers
Text copyright © 1994 Duncan Baird Publishers
Commissioned artwork and photographs copyright © 1994 Duncan Baird Publishers
For copyright of other illustrations, see page 40
All rights reserved. No part of this book may be reproduced without written permission from the Publisher.

A DBP Book, conceived, edited and designed by
Duncan Baird Publishers
Castle House
75-76 Wells Street
London
W1P 3RE

Text: *Kate Langley*
Design: *Karen Wilks*
Commissioned artwork: *Hannah Firmin*
Picture research: *Julia Brown*
Additional research: *Lucy Curtin*

1 3 5 7 9 10 8 6 4 2

Library of Congress Cataloging-in-Publication Data:
Magic: a book of symbols.
p.   cm. — (Prospero's library)
ISBN 0-8118-1042-9
1. Symbolism. 2. Magic. I. Series.
BF1623.S9M34   1995
133.4'3—dc20   94-37303
CIP

Distributed in Canada by Raincoast Books,
8680 Cambie Street, Vancouver, B.C. V6P 6M9

Chronicle Books
275 Fifth Street
San Francisco, California 94103

Printed in Hong Kong

CONTENTS

The circle of the spirit

In magic (which may be defined as the process and practice of spiritual and material transformation), the circle is the most universal of all symbols. As an unbroken line it represents perfection, eternity and the never-ending cycle of creation, decay and regeneration. The ancient magical writings called the *Hermetica* (*c.*AD 150) describe the divine creator spirit as a circle with its circumference nowhere and its centre everywhere.

Divided circle
A circle divided horizontally represents the dynamic polarity underlying magical transformation: the lower state of hidden potential and the higher state of exaltation and enlightenment. The artist, poet and mystic William Blake (1757–1827) presented this polarity as the biblical monsters Behemoth and Leviathan.

Three circles entwined
A triplet of interlaced circles symbolizes the mystical union of male, female and spirit, itself derived from the sacred union of Father, Son and Holy Ghost. In Chinese magic this symbol represents the triad of heaven, earth and humanity.

The language of magic

Tai-chi

The tai-chi is a circle enclosing the *yin* and *yang*, the two opposing but complementary forces of creation. Surrounding the tai-chi are the Eight Trigrams, magic symbols used in Chinese divination to determine the balance of cosmic forces at any one time.

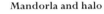

Mandorla and halo

Two circles overlap to create the mandorla ("almond"). This magic symbol represents the interpenetration of the material and immaterial worlds: here it encloses the figure of Christ, the divine spirit made flesh. His head is surrounded by a halo, a radiant circle representing divine enlightenment and transfiguration.

Radiant circle

A symbol of the sun as a source of life and heat and as an agent of magical transmutation. The flaming heart at the centre is the fiery transcendent power of God, from whom supreme creative force emanates.

✳

6

The language of magic

The quadrant of matter

If the circle is the emblem of
the infinite and spiritual, the
figure with four sides of fixed
length represents stability, order
and the finite material world.
For the ancient Greeks, the
square symbolized the powers
of the love goddess Aphrodite.

Lozenge

In Western magic, the lozenge or diamond
– a square balanced precariously on one
corner – denotes volatility, the fluidity of
the spirit within matter. In the East, it is a
form of the *yoni*, a symbol of regeneration
derived from the female genitals.

Circle in the square

According to Oriental magicians, the square enclosing a circle is an emblem of a person's whole being: making contact with the eternal spirit (the circle) within the mortal body (the square) is the starting point for magical transformation.

Microcosmic man

The 16th-century German magician Cornelius Agrippa presented the figure of a man within a square (above) as a microcosm of the finite world and the four elements: Earth (flesh), Air (breath), Fire (body heat) and Water (blood).

The language of magic

The sacral triangle

For magicians the universe is governed by the principle of three, which the Greek philosopher Aristotle called "the number of the Whole, that which has within itself beginning, middle and end". The triangle often represents cosmic trinities arising from this principle, such as birth, life and death or Father, Son and Holy Ghost.

Seal of Solomon

The star formed of two interlaced triangles (right) was reputedly the magic seal of King Solomon of Israel (*c*.950 BC), who is said to have used it to control demons and genies. The seal denotes the indissoluble union of heaven and earth and also (left) the dual nature of Christ as man and deity (the four-petalled rose stands for the Crucifixion). It is also believed to ward off fire and may be worn as an amulet (see opposite, above right) to avert the evil eye.

Downward-pointing triangle

This symbol represents the moon and the
feminine creative principle (it resembles the
female pudenda). It also stands for water and the
introspective temperament: "still waters run deep".

Pyramid

Uniting the triangle and the square in
three dimensions, the Egyptian pyramid
symbolizes the apex of spiritual and
physical renewal. This stepped pyramid
(left) represents ascending levels of
consciousness leading to the highest
celestial state. Imhotep, an architect also
famed as a magician, built it as the tomb
of the Pharaoh Djoser (*c.*2650 BC).

Upward-pointing triangle

The triangle pointing heavenward is a symbol of the rising
sun and represents a striving after the celestial and divine.
It also stands for flame and the extrovert temperament.
As an emblem of the phallus, it denotes the masculine
creative principle.

The cross of renewal

The cross combines horizontal and vertical elements, which can be seen as representing cosmic opposites such as heaven and earth, life and death, light and dark. It may also denote the ancient concept of the tree of life: in pre-Christian Europe the cross was often linked with the worship of nature.

Christian cross

The Christian cross (below) symbolizes the

transformation of humanity through the death and resurrection of Christ. It is widely used as a magic charm: English bakers once marked loaves with a cross to stop the devil from sitting on them and preventing the dough from rising.

Labarum

The Greeks saw the labarum, an ancient sacred talisman, as a combination of chi (χ) and rho (ρ), the first letters of *chreston* ("a good sign"). Later, it came to stand for Christ (right).

Ankh

The Egyptian cross of life, the ankh, combines solar, phallic and vaginal symbolism. It represents sacred lore and wisdom

acquired through magical initiation. A chain of ankhs surrounds the central figure (above).

Celtic cross

Predating Christianity by at least 1,500 years, the Celtic cross (left) may have originated as the stylized spokes and rim of a wheel – an emblem of the sun and the life-giving power of the solar deity. It was used as a charm to placate supernatural forces and as a protective amulet in battle.

Swastika

Perhaps a whirling sun symbol in origin, the swastika (left) occurs in lands as far apart as the ancient Middle East and the Americas to denote good fortune, health and prosperity. It is especially common in India, where householders paint it on the threshold to ward off evil.

The all-seeing eye

Linking the outer material world and the inner life of the spirit, the eye is the pathway for wisdom and enlightenment. But it may also be a channel for darker forces, reflected in the old belief in the "evil eye" – the ability to transmit curses and misfortune through a single glance.

Eye of providence

One common magic emblem is the radiant eye of providence, invoking divine insight and heavenly protection. On the Great Seal of the United States (above right), it oversees the building of the pyramid, the symbol of the nation and its spiritual aspirations.

Third eye

The Hindu god Shiva possesses a third eye, or *shakra*, in his forehead. It represents transcendent wisdom, supernatural vision and enlightenment – but also the deity's power of destruction.

Eye of Horus

The Eye of Horus or *wedjat* was one of the most sacred symbols in ancient Egyptian magic. It represents the omnipresence and vigilance of the sky god Horus, who oversees the destiny of humanity, radiating benefit from his right eye (the sun) and his left eye (the moon). In this devotional painting of *c.*1000 BC (left), two *wedjats* appear at the top alongside ankh crosses and other magic emblems.

Eye of wisdom

The Islamic amulet (below) presents the eye as a spiritual gateway (the almond-shaped mandorla) leading directly to the soul (the circle). Within this is a smaller circle that is the individual's true spiritual centre, the receptacle of divine knowledge.

The power of numbers

The ancient Greeks believed that numbers were magical principles governing the entire universe, with the number one as the spirit from which everything arose. Jewish magicians assigned every name a numerical equivalent, to which they attributed great mystical significance: for example, the number of God was eight.

Alchemical duality

In alchemy, two represents the fusion of opposing elements, symbolized by the androgyne (above). The dragon's wings denote the state of conflict preceding the achievement of harmony.

Cosmic trinity

Three denotes any cosmic whole made up of a trinity, such as time (past, present, future). For French kings the trefoil lily (left) symbolized the Holy Trinity and the mystical union of God, king and soil. Turning around three times is one traditional way to avert the evil eye.

Four

The four-leafed design within a square (left) stands for the transcendent cross of Christ and His word (the four gospels) binding the four corners of the world. The five-petalled rose is Christ Himself, who suffered five wounds on the cross.

Pentagram

The five-pointed star, or pentagram, is the symbol of five-limbed Man or Woman. It also represents the Quintessence, the mystical fifth element. The inverted pentagram resembles the horns, ears and face of the Devil: it is used in black magic.

Seven

The seven-headed dragon (left) personifies the Seven Deadly Sins and the seven devils cast out by Christ. In folk magic, seven is usually a lucky number. A seventh child, it is said, possesses the power to foretell the future and cure disease.

The elements

Alchemists believed that the primal matter which underwent magical transformation was composed of four elements, Earth, Air, Fire and Water, which combine in countless ways to produce everything in nature. They are bound by a mystical fifth element known as the Quintessence.

Fire

The red triangle and volcano represent Fire, the consuming element. It is associated with the zodiacal fire sign of Leo and with St. Mark, whose emblem is the lion.

Air

A blue or gold triangle is Air, the volatile element. It is associated with the air sign Aquarius and with St. Matthew, who is symbolized by the water carrier.

The four humours

The elements had their counterpart in the humours, substances which made up the human body (clockwise from top left): Phlegm (equated with Water), Blood (Air), Choler (Fire) and Black Bile or Melancholia (Earth). Depending on their predominant humour, people were said to be phlegmatic, sanguine, choleric or melancholic.

Water

An inverted blue triangle is Water, the fluid element. It is associated with the water sign Scorpio and with St. John the Evangelist, whose emblem is the eagle.

Earth

The inverted green triangle is Earth, the stable element. It is associated with the earth sign Taurus and with St. Luke, whose emblem is the bull.

The power of nature

Places of enchantment

Many natural features are revered as manifestations of the earth spirit which possess a magical aura. Travellers who passed at night through an oak grove were once warned against the spirits of the old felled oaks, which sought revenge on humans for being cut down. Elder trees, on the other hand, gave protection from witches and malign spirits.

Sacred grove

The Druids, magician-priests of the ancient Celts, believed that the protective deities and spirits of trees set aside groves and clearings (above) as places for their worship. It is said that if you try to count the trees encircling a grove, the tree spirits will make you lose count.

Standing stones

Prehistoric standing stones are sometimes said to be people who have been turned to rock for some transgression. In other traditions stones have magical healing properties, relieving rheumatism and bestowing fertility on barren women who visit them at midnight.

Wishing well

In Scotland, anyone who wanted a wish
to come true would go to a sacred well
before sunrise, walk around it three
times, dip a scrap of cloth in the water
and tie the cloth to the branch of a tree.

Fairy hawthorn

A green branch cut from the hawthorn (or
may) will keep mischievous fairies from the
house on Mayday eve – as long as it bears no
white blossom, which attracts Death. A may
tree standing alone or in a ring of three is
reputed to be the meeting place of fairies.

Tree man

Immobile by day, trees were once
reputed to walk abroad like humans
after dark. Willows, it was said,
especially enjoyed shuffling along,
grumbling as they went, behind
terrified lone travellers.

The power of nature

Magic plants

When Shakespeare referred to "the powerful Grace that lies in plants" he was reflecting a traditional belief in the magical properties of plants and flowers. This faith, which persists to this day, is very ancient: the Romans, for example, believed that laurel averted thunder and lightning.

Mistletoe
The Druids gathered mistletoe with great reverence, cutting it from sacred oaks on the full moon with a golden sickle. The plant was said to protect against fire and flood, and as part of a magic potion it was also believed to cure infertility.

Daffodil
In some Celtic regions, the daffodil was thought to transmit a powerful magic that rendered beasts infertile. Farmers would not have them in the house while geese, ducks or chickens were laying eggs, for fear that none of them would hatch.

Fern

Fern spores gathered at midnight on the eve of the feast of St. John the Baptist is said to make a person invisible. In Wales, wagoners carried a bunch of fern to confound witches.

Harebell

To know when she will wed, a maiden must pick the first harebells of spring and invoke the grace of fairies. The number of flowers will then equal the years she must wait for a husband.

Peyotl

Aboriginal American traditions recognize many plants with supernatural properties (left). For the Aztecs and other peoples, the most potent was peyotl or peyote, a cactus plant that was said to confer long life.

The fish of transfiguration

The fish is an almost universal symbol of water as a source of fertility and renewed life. In Western Christian traditions it is the emblem of the resurrected Christ: the first letters of "Jesus Christ, Son of God, Saviour" in Greek spell the word *ichthus* ("fish").

Three fishes
A symbol of Christian baptism, during which both body and spirit undergo a magical transformation. After passing through the holy water of life, they emerge in the grace of the Trinity.

Jonah

Medieval magicians interpreted the story of Jonah as a metaphor for the transfiguration of the human spirit. Fleeing from God, Jonah is consumed by the watery darkness of chaos (the belly of a "great fish" – not necessarily a whale). Three days later, he emerges into the light, prepared to do God's will.

Two fishes

In China, as elsewhere, the fish represents abundance and fertility. A pair of fishes depicted with a house (right) symbolizes fruitful union and is found as an amulet to ensure marital bliss.

Fisherman's amulet

For at least 2,500 years, fishermen in the Mediterranean have painted fish-eye talismans (left) on the prows of their vessels. They are believed to grant the boat the ability to see the best location for a good haul of fish.

The mystic serpent

Serpents, which dwell unseen beneath the earth, often symbolize occult knowledge. Two entwined serpents represent the light and dark sides of the mind, knowledge and intuition. The eagle with a snake in its mouth stands for the triumph of higher instincts over low impulses or, in alchemical terms, the liberation of divine essence from base matter.

Serpent on cross
The serpent attached to a cross or tree represents the alchemical process of *fixatio*, whereby the burning principle (called "sulphur") fixes the volatile principle ("quicksilver" or "mercury"). The crown on the serpent's head denotes the ultimate spiritual knowledge attained once *fixatio* has been achieved.

Caduceus

The caduceus (right), formed
from two snakes around a central
staff and crowned by a pair of wings,
is the wand of Hermes, the Greek god of
Magic. The snakes represent cosmic dualities
such as good and evil. The staff denotes
the reconciliation of such opposites by
magical powers ultimately derived from
heaven (symbolized by the wings).

Coiled serpent

The spiralled snake
embodies pent-up
creative energy.
However, it is also
a vortex and may
be a source of
destruction.

Makers of magic

Magicians trace their profession
back thousands of years to historical
figures such as King Solomon.
Recent practitioners, including
Eliphas Lévi (1810–1875) and
Aleister Crowley (1875–1947),
have further developed the
magical tradition.

Agrippa
In his book
*On Occult
Philosophy* the
German magician
Cornelius Agrippa
(1486–1535)
developed many of
the symbols still
employed by
magicians and
astrologers,

Thoth
The Egyptian deity of magic was the ibis-headed
moon god Thoth (above), who was worshipped at
Khemenu. He is said to have written the first book of
magical lore, the location of which remains hidden to this day.

for example
those for the
signs of the
Zodiac (clockwise
from top of page):
Aries, Taurus,
Gemini, Cancer,
Leo, Virgo, Libra,
Scorpio, Sagittarius,
Capricorn,
Aquarius
and Pisces.

Hermes
The Greeks identified Thoth with
the god Hermes (above). Magicians
call him Hermes Trismegistus
("Thrice great Hermes") and credit
him with the authorship of the
Hermetica, ancient writings that are
the prime source of European
magical traditions.

Magic monad
The magician John Dee
(1527–1608) devised the
"Monad", a complex symbol
for the primal essence of the
manifested world. It combines the
Moon (crescent), the Sun (circle with dot),
the Elements (cross) and Fire (the fire sign Aries).

The magical arts

Witchcraft

Witches – practitioners of pagan magic – are not always malevolent. Nevertheless, they are said to conjure up thunderstorms by combing their hair and the Hallowe'en custom of "trick or treat" has its origins in the belief that gifts must be left to placate demonic spirits raised by witchcraft. A witch can assume many animal forms, especially that of a cat.

Rangda
Balinese dancers re-enact the struggle between the evil witch Rangda (above) and Barong, leader of the forces of good. Rangda may be based on a real 11th-century queen who was exiled for sorcery.

Baba Iaga
The witch of Slav folklore is the Baba Iaga, a hideous crone who lives in a dark forest inside a hut that stands on chickens' legs. She is usually malevolent but sometimes fights monsters such as the dragon-like "crocodile" (above, left).

Witch's garden

The young woman (right) looks innocent, but the plants scattered on the floor include henbane, hemlock and deadly nightshade (or belladonna) – potent hallucinogens used by witches. This witch's familiar is a white dog: white is often associated with magic.

Witch of Okabe

In Japanese legend, the witch Yoshifuji assumed the form of a monstrous cat to frighten young women who visited a temple on the road to Tokkaido. Yoshifuji was eventually overcome by her own magic and turned to stone.

Hare

According to Celtic tradition, a witch will often take the form of a hare to sneak into fields and suck the milk from cows. Once, in parts of Ireland, any hare seen on May 1st was regarded as a witch and stoned to death.

The magic of the Orient

The tales gathered together in *The 1001 Nights* contain many accounts of transformations, levitations, monsters and spirits. Although told within an Islamic context, these stories often reflect beliefs in the supernatural that predate the advent of Muhammad (*c.*570–632 AD).

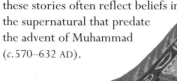

Magic carpet
Carpets possessing the ability to levitate are common in Arabian myth. The original flying carpet, it is said, belonged to King Solomon and was big enough to carry his army.

Genies

The genie (left), a supernatural being below the level of the angels and devils, was made of air or flame and could adopt any human or animal form. Genies caused all kinds of illnesses and accidents, but they could be controlled through certain magical formulas. King Solomon is said to have trapped genies in sealed vessels and hurled them into the sea.

Ifrits and ghouls

Ifrits are huge winged demons made of smoke (left). Strong and cunning, they live underground and in old ruins. Ghouls, shape-changing spirits who inhabit cemeteries, stalk the desert in the guise of beautiful women to waylay travellers and eat them. However, ghouls can always be detected by their ass's hooves.

Hand of Fatima

In Islamic tradition no woman was more virtuous than Fatima, the daughter of the Prophet Muhammad. Charms representing her raised hand are worn to ward off the evil eye.

Magical metamorphosis

Stories of transformation through magic abound in myth and folklore. The belief that anyone who strayed into fairy territory risked being turned into stone or into an animal was once so strong in Ireland and Scotland that people respectfully referred to fairies as "good neighbours".

Reynard's magic ring

Reynard the Fox (below), the wily hero of medieval European folktale, claimed to know of a magic gold ring bearing three mysterious Hebrew words. The ring rendered Reynard invisible and protected him from witchcraft. It had one unusual property: it existed only in his imagination.

Philosopher's Stone

Alchemists sought the "Philosopher's Stone", a medium – solid or liquid – that could transform spirit and matter into a state of ultimate perfection. Its discovery would be signalled by the transmutation of lead into gold.

Cloak of invisibility
Charged with slaying the Gorgon Medusa, whose stare turned anything to stone, the Greek hero Perseus went to certain nymphs for assistance. They gave him a cloak that made him invisible, allowing him to approach the monster unseen and cut off her head (left).

Elixir of life
Chinese myth tells of the lady Chang E, who acquired a magical elixir that would grant her eternal life in the heavens. An astrologer told her to go to the moon, where she would be magically transformed. Chang E took the elixir, flew to the moon – and turned into a toad.

The power of foreseeing

From the earliest times people have sought ways of divining what the future holds. Astrology is probably the most popular method of prediction in both the West and the East, but there are countless other traditions. For example, certain plants (such as mugwort) are said to bestow prophetic powers on those who consume them.

Palmistry

Palmists ascribe a special divinatory significance to every finger, line and mound on the hand: a wedding ring is worn on the third finger because a powerful line of energy is said to connect this finger to the heart.

Oracle bones

Pieces of bone with magical markings (left) are widely used for divination throughout southern Africa. Each bone has a "positive" (patterned) side and a "negative" (blank) side. They are cast by a diviner who interprets the combination of positives and negatives: if all the bones are positive, the client is overactive and should take life a little bit easier.

Runes

The ancient Germanic letters called runes were also powerful magic symbols. They were used for divination and to make contact with hidden spiritual wisdom (rune is said to mean "mystery"). Inscribed on sticks (right) or stones, runes are cast onto a special runic diagram: a reading is taken from the pattern in which they land.

Candle burning blue

A lighted candle is said to burn blue when a spirit — maybe Death itself — is in the house or not far from it. The danger can be averted by extinguishing the candle in running water.

Tarot

The Tarot was simply a set of playing cards until the 18th century, when magicians first interpreted the cards as a complex divination system derived from ancient lore. New symbolic meanings were attached to the cards, which include (left to right, above): the Juggler ("willpower"); the High Priestess ("knowledge"); the Emperor ("achievement"); and the Lovers ("aspiration").

The healing spirit

Hippocrates (c. 300 BC), the great Greek physician, believed that some people possessed a magical aura that enabled them to heal sickness. Animals are often associated with curing powers: warts were once said to disappear after being rubbed with a snail that was then impaled on a hawthorn, a tree with ancient magical associations.

Pig

In parts of Ireland, if a child contracted mumps, its nurse would wrap the youngster in a blanket and stroke its head against a pig. The disease was said to pass magically from child to animal.

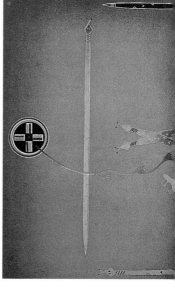

Abracadabra

This formula may be a corruption of the spell *abbada ke dabra* ("perish as the word") from ancient Chaldea (now Iraq). It was believed that a fever would vanish if the word was repeated with one letter left off each time, until only "A" remained. Written down (right), the spell guarded against illness.

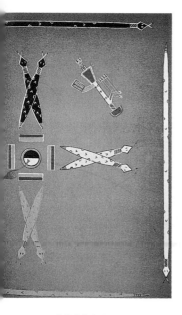

Sandpainting

Navajo shamans use sandpaintings, depictions of sacred myths made in sand with coloured powders, in their curing rituals. The patient enters the painting and becomes a character in the myth: the experience is believed to restore his or her harmony with the spirit world, ensuring a return to health.

ABRACADABRA
ABRACADABR
ABRACADAB
ABRACADA
ABRACAD
ABRACA
ABRAC
ABRA
ABR
AB
A

Piebald horse

Traditionally a lucky animal, the black and white horse is also credited with the ability to cure whooping cough, especially in Celtic regions. Cornish custom requires the sufferer to pass under its belly three times, while in Wales the patient must inhale its breath.

Charms and amulets

Since ancient times people have valued certain objects as magical charms against misfortune. Traditional amulets include the foot of a hare or rabbit (animals associated with witchcraft) and the four-leafed clover, which makes fairies visible and wards off their spells.

Abraxas stone
The Gnostics, members of an influential mystical movement which flourished *c.*150 AD, inscribed Greek letters on stone as magical charms. The stones were sacred to Abraxas, the divine personification of magical and esoteric knowledge.

Garlic
Irish countryfolk formerly planted cloves of wild garlic in the thatch over their front doors to bring good luck. In Slav lands, garlic was renowned for its power to ward off vampires, werewolves and other evil spirits.

Shaman's charm
Native American shamans often used small bone amulets to represent the creatures from which they derived their magical powers. This Tsimshian amulet is a hybrid of a human and a bird, possibly a crane.

Basmallah
The most powerful amulet for Muslims is the Basmallah, the invocation "In the name of God, the Merciful, the Compassionate" (left). According to Arabian magical tradition it was inscribed on Adam's flank, Gabriel's wing, Solomon's seal and Christ's tongue.

Household amulet
Representing the union of heaven (the circle) and earth (the square), the Chinese bronze amulet (left) is hung in the home to bring the four blessings expressed in the characters it bears: good fortune, health, wealth and happiness.

Acknowledgments

The publishers are grateful to the following for permission to
reproduce their photographs:

Key: b: bottom c: centre l: left r: right t: top

Page 4:(t) (*The Book of Job*, detail, by W. Blake) Charles Walker Collection/
Images, London; 4:(b) Charles Walker Collection/Images; 5:(t) Charles
Walker Collection/Images; 5:(c) The British Library, London/ The
Bridgeman Art Library, London; 7: Charles Walker Collection/Images; 8:(t)
Charles Walker Collection/ Images;8:(b) Charles Walker Collection; 9:(t)
Tariq Rajab Museum, Kuwait/Charles Walker Collection/Images; 9:(b)
Silvio Fiore/The Bridgeman Art Library; 10:(l) Lambeth Palace Library,
London/The Bridgeman Art Library; 10:(r) Dorset Country Museum/The
Bridgeman Art Library;11: Musée du Louvre, Paris/Giraudon, Paris/The
Bridgeman Art Library; 12: The Victoria & Albert Museum, London/The
Bridgeman Art Library; 13:(t) Musée du Louvre/Giraudon/The Bridgeman
Art Library; 13:(b) Dar al Athar al Islammiyyah, Kuwait/Charles Walker
Collection/Images;14:(c) Charles Walker Collection/Images; 14:(b)
Bibliothèque Nationale, Paris/The Bridgeman Art Library; 15: Winchelsea
Church, Sussex/Charles Walker Collection/Images; 17: Charles Walker
Collection/Images; 18: Piper Stones, Co. Wicklow/Images; 19: Julia Simon
Fine Art Ltd/The Bridgeman Art Library; 20:(t) Private Collection/The
Bridgeman Art Library; 20:(b) The Fitzwilliam Museum, Cambridge/The
Bridgeman Art Library; 21:(tl) The Victoria & Albert Museum/The
Bridgeman Art Library; 21:(tr) The Lindley Library, Royal Horticultural
Society, London/The Bridgeman Art Library; 21:(b) Vatican Museum &
Galleries, Rome/The Bridgeman Art Library; 23:(t) St. Etienne Church,
Mulhouse/Charles Walker Collection/Images; 23:(b) Charles Walker
Collection/Images; 25:(t) Bonham's, London/The Bridgeman Art Library;
25:(b) Private Collection, London/Charles Walker Collection/ Images; 26:
Charles Walker Collection/Images; 27: Museo Nazionale, Taranto/DBP
Archive; 28: Museum of Mankind, The British Museum, London/Michael
Holford, London; 29:(t) (*The Withcraft of Love,* Anon. *c.*1500) Museum der
Bildenden Künste, Leipzig/The Bridgeman Art Library; 29:(b) Private
Collection/E.T. Archive, London; 30: Musée du Louvre/Giraudon/The
Bridgeman Art Library; 31:(t) The British Library/The Bridgeman Art
Library; 31:(b) Tariq Rajab Museum/Charles Walker Collection/Images; 32:
The British Library/The Bridgeman Art Library; 33: The British
Museum/The Bridgeman Art Library; 34:(c) The British Museum/DBP
Archive; 34:(b) The British Museum/Michael Holford; 35:(t) Private
Collection/Charles Walker Collection/Images; 35:(c) The British
Museum/DBP Archive; 36/37: Michael Holford; 37: (*Charivari,* detail. by
L. Knight) Newport Museum & Art Galleries, Gwent; 38: Charles Walker
Collection/Images; 39:(t) Provincial Museum, Victoria, British Columbia/
Werner Forman Archive, London; 39:(c) Charles Walker Collection/
Images; 39:(b) CharlesWalker Collection/Images.